ork

Motorcycles

by Allan Morey

Bullfrog Books

Ideas for Parents and Teachers

Bullfrog Books let children practice nonfiction reading at the earliest reading levels. Repetition, familiar words, and photo labels support early readers.

Before Reading

- Discuss the cover photo. What does it tell them?
- Look at the picture glossary together. Read and discuss the words.

Read the Book

- "Walk" through the book and look at the photos. Let the child ask questions. Point out the photo labels.
- Read the book to the child, or have him or her read independently.

After Reading

- Prompt the child to think more. Ask: Where have you seen a motorcycle? Who was riding it? Where do you think they were going?

Bullfrog Books are published by Jump!
5357 Penn Avenue South
Minneapolis, MN 55419
www.jumplibrary.com

Copyright © 2015 Jump! International copyright reserved in all countries. No part of this book may be reproduced in any form without written permission from the publisher.

Library of Congress Cataloging-in-Publication Data

Morey, Allan.
  Motorcycles / by Allan Morey.
    pages cm — (Bullfrog books. Machines at work)
  Includes bibliographical references and index.
  Summary: "This photo-illustrated book for early readers tells about the different kinds of motorcycles that people ride and what those bikes are used for" — Provided by publisher.
  ISBN 978-1-62031-103-5 (hardcover) —
  ISBN 978-1-62496-171-7 (ebook)
  1. Motorcycles — Juvenile literature. I. Title.
  TL440.15.M65 2015
  629.227'5—dc23
                              2013039881

Series Editor: Wendy Dieker
Series Designer: Ellen Huber
Book Designer: Anna Peterson
Photo Researcher: Kurtis Kinneman

Photo Credits: Alamy/Lars Nilseng, 18–19; Alamy/Oleksiy Maksymenko Photography, 17, 23bl; American Honda Motor, 10–11, 23br; Dreamstime.com/Mlan61, 22; iStock/kinemero, 14 (inset); Mat Smith, 12–13, 23tr; Shutterstock/Brian McEntire, 1; Shutterstock/John Roman Images, 16; Shutterstock/Maxx-Studio, 9; Thinkstock/Jupiterimages, 8; © 2014 Yamaha Motor Corporation, U.S.A. All rights reserved., cover, 3, 4, 5, 6–7, 13 (inset), 14–15, 20–21, 23tl, 24

Printed in the United States of America at Corporate Graphics, in North Mankato, Minnesota.
3-2014
10 9 8 7 6 5 4 3 2 1

Table of Contents

Vroom! Vroom!

Do you hear that?

It is a motorcycle.

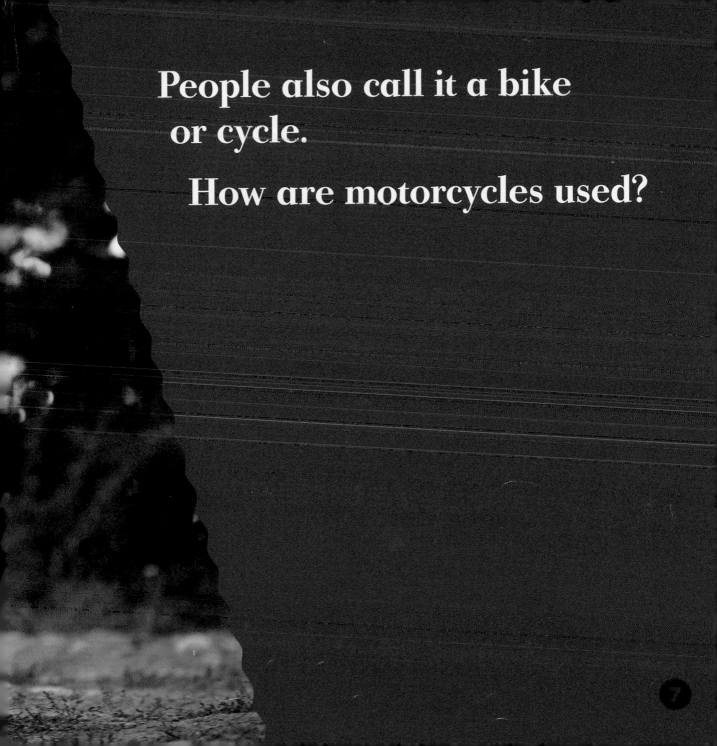

People also call it a bike
or cycle.

How are motorcycles used?

Sue rides one to work.

It is smaller than a car.

It uses less gas.

Tom goes on a long trip.

He rides a touring bike.

Jim races a superbike.

It has smooth tires.

They help it go fast.

Zoom!

smooth tire

A dirt bike has knobby tires.

Ben races in mud.

He jumps over hills.

knobby
tire

Pam is a
police officer.

Her cycle has a siren.

The lights flash.

The police drive
by the beach.

Their cycles go where
a police car can't go.

John and Addie
ride just for fun.

Whee!

Parts of a Motorcycle

helmet
This protects a rider's head in case of an accident.

throttle
This lets gas into the engine so the motorcycle can go faster.

windshield
This protects a rider from bugs and other flying objects while riding.

foot peg
A place for a rider to rest his or her foot while riding.

Picture Glossary

dirt bike
A motorcycle with knobby tires that is used on dirt tracks.

superbike
A motorcycle with extra power and smooth tires, used for racing.

police motorcycle
A motorcycle that has lights and a siren like a police car.

touring bike
A big motorcycle used on long trips.

Index

To Learn More

Learning more is as easy as 1, 2, 3.

1) Go to www.factsurfer.com

2) Enter "motorcycle" into the search box.

3) Click the "Surf" button to see a list of websites.

With factsurfer.com, finding more information is just a click away.